May the Lord give might to
His people; may the Lord bless
His people with peace!
Psalm 29:11

The intent and
purpose of this volume is to
give you faith, hope and
inspiration. Hopefully it will help bring
peace and tranquility into your life. May
it be a reminder of God's love, guidance
and His many blessings.

Our publications help to support our work
for needy children in over 120 countries
around the world. Through our
programs, thousands of children are
fed, clothed, educated, sheltered
and given the opportunity to
live decent lives.

Salesian Missions wishes to extend special thanks and gratitude to our generous poet friends and to the publishers who have given us permission to reprint material included in this book. Every effort has been made to give proper acknowledgments. Any omissions or errors are deeply regretted, and the publisher, upon notification, will be pleased to make the necessary corrections in subsequent editions.

Cover photo: ©Stockbyte Photography/Fotosearch.com

First Edition Printed in the U.S.A. by Concord Litho Group, Concord, NH 03301.

Blessed Peace
from the Salesian Collection

Compiled and Edited
by Jennifer Grimaldi

Illustrated by
Robert VanSteinburg, Russell Bushée,
Paul Scully, Frank Massa, Dorian Remine,
Terrie Meider and Maureen McCarthy

Contents

5

God's Loving Gifts

Each season brings a special joy
To those who care to see
The wonders of God's handiwork
And awesome majesty.

Each Spring brings birth, a greening earth,
And robins on the wing,
As hyacinths and daffodils
Stir hearts and make them sing.

Each Summer, Fall and Winter, too,
Brings joy and wonderment
At all the loving gifts bestowed
Throughout God's firmament.

Vi B. Chevalier

Once Upon
An April Day

Once upon an April day,
Robins chirped a roundelay.
Tulips drenched in morning dew
Dazzled me in their debut.

Once upon an April day,
Flowers bloomed in full array.
Golden beams of sunlight spilled
Upon my garden daffodilled.

Once upon an April day,
Thunderclouds came out to play.
And after raindrops tumbled down,
April wore a rainbow crown.

Nora M. Bozeman

*Indeed, before You the whole
universe is as a grain from a
balance, or a drop of morning
dew come down upon the earth.*
Wisdom 11:22

The Walk

I took a walk with the Lord today
Just to talk things over.
I ambled through His fields of green
With springtime clumps of clover.
I told Him all my troubles plain
And all I thought was wrong,
But He replied, "Fear not, My child,
I'm with you all along."
I looked around at all He'd made,
And marveled mountain's height,
And burdens seemed to vanish there –
Was quite a welcomed sight.
The flowers budding fresh with blooms
All gloriously covered,
With splendid colored butterflies
And birds in graceful hover.

He showed His face in Nature's beauty,
His love in Spring's returning.
And I was blessed by this display,
My heart with deeper yearning.
So take a walk and tarry
Just to feel God's loving arms,
Holding you, embracing you,
Releasing healing calm.

Lynda Bryan Davis

*Fear not, I am with you; be not
dismayed; I am your God. I
will strengthen you, and help
you, and uphold you with My
right hand of justice.*
Isaiah 41:10

His Touch

He is in the silent night,
I can see Him all around,
I can feel His grace and goodness,
Though I hear not a sound.

I can see Him in all places,
By the miracles that be,
In the mountains high and wide,
In the deep, blue sea.

He is with me in the garden,
Near the trees majestic, high,
In the grass beneath my feet,
In the deep and purple sky.

He permeates all spaces –
His loving, sweet embrace.
When I caressed a flower,
It seems I touched His face.

James Joseph Huesgen

Majestic and glorious is
Your work, Your wise
design endures forever.
Psalm 111:3

When God Looks Down and Smiles

A golden-yellow sun comes up
And birds begin to sing,
A rose puts forth its fragrant bloom,
A butterfly spreads its wings…
A gentle rain refreshes the earth,
A rainbow appears in the sky,
A mother horse bears a colt,
An eagle soars on high…
All the earth gives glory to God,
Each man and woman and child,
And all proclaim His wondrous deeds…
As God looks down and smiles.

Steven Michael Schumacher

*Sing to Him, sing His
praise, proclaim all His
wondrous deeds.*
1 Chronicles 16:9

The Beauty God Sends My Way

I stroll within the garden
Each morn that I arise,
Admiring the beauty
Displayed before my eyes…

Clumps of daisies planted here,
Poppies planted yon,
A row of mini-sunflowers
With faces toward the sun.

A birdbath filled with water
In one small garden nook,
Birds and butterflies a-wing,
Which I can't overlook.

A minute wooden birdhouse,
A home for little wrens;
Another house for bluebirds
Down at the garden's end.

An arbor wrapped with roses
That bloom the Summer through,
A fountain midst the florets,
So lovely to the view.

I stroll within the garden
At dawning of the day
To thank God for the beauty
That He has sent my way.

Loise Pinkerton Fritz

*He hath made everything
beautiful in His time…*
Ecclesiastes 3:11

13

Dear God...

Please open my ears
That I might hear
Your tender, loving voice.

Open my eyes
To see You near
And teach me to rejoice.

Help me know
The power I have
Through Jesus Christ, my Lord.

Help others to hear
The song of my heart
Because of the One I adore.

Sharon Fuqua

Offering

Early in the morning
Before the start of day,
I pause to savor sunrise
And stop for time to pray.

The birds wake up and visit,
Their singing paints the air;
Flowers open to the sun,
My heart whispers a prayer.

Thanksgiving to a loving God
Who knows my wants and needs,
Who gives me everything that's good;
I follow where He leads.

My heart is His and His alone
Each day from start to end;
I offer everything I do
To God, who is my Friend.

Delphine LeDoux

*May this prayer I have
offered to the Lord, our
God, be present to Him
day and night…*
1 Kings 8:59

Thank You

Lord, I thank You for this day,
And all that will ensue.
I pray that all I say and do
Will bring glory unto You.

Inspire every word I say
And guard my actions, too.
Show me the path You'd have me take
And what You'd have me do.

May I be a beacon,
Sharing Your love today,
Reaching, ever reaching out
With You guiding my way.

Dona M. Maroney

Quiet

If the world were still and silent,
No music would be heard –
There would be no children's laughter,
Nor song of Summer bird.
No one would hear leaves rustle,
Nor would the thunder sound –
No moving brooks would babble –
No ocean waves resound.
If all the world were silent,
Mankind would feel it odd
To not hear joy or sadness,
And the whispering of God.

Joan Stephen

*They found abundant and good
pastures, and the land was
spacious, quiet and peaceful.*
1 Chronicles 4:40

His Wonders

He clothes the world with beauty,
With flowers, grass and trees.
The mountains stand in majesty,
Looking down on rolling seas.

Blue skies above, a canvas
For sunset's flaming hues,
Proclaim a wondrous God
Whose love is ever true.

His word to guide our living,
That leads us all life long,
Brings peace to troubled hearts
And on our lips a song.

We feast upon His wonders
And beauty unsurpassed,
A preview of what is to come
When we reach home at last.

His wonders speak of Heaven,
Worth more than earthly fame,
To share when days on earth are done,
For all who love His name.

Helen Gleason

No Greater
Love Than God's Love

God's love resembles the sunshine –
Ever glowing and lighting the way,
Providing the warmth of its presence
And helping us greet the day.
God's love is like the rushing tides
And spans the ocean wide.
It also can adjust the size
To fit a wee heart inside.
His love resembles the song of a bird,
Chirping a sweet springtime melody;
It's the beautiful world around us –
Every flower, rainbow, and tree.
God's love is often like a lighthouse –
Guiding and pointing the way
To a brighter, more peaceful tomorrow
And a much happier today.
There's no greater love than God's love
And He offers it to you and to me;
It comforts amid life's sorrows
And from sin it sets us free.

Linda C. Grazulis

Walk Through This World
With Me, Lord

Walk through this world with me, Lord,
Stay close by my side.
I need You to guide my way, Lord,
Whatever betide.

My life is an unknown path, Lord,
And the way I cannot see.
So, please take my hand, Lord,
And walk through this world with me.

Shirley W. Langley

For I the Lord, thy God, will hold
thy right hand saying unto thee,
fear not; I will keep thee.
Isaiah 41:13

Gifts of Beauty

So many gifts of beauty
I find along my day,
Each one a masterpiece of art
For which I do not pay.

The rose-pink mist of early dawn,
A butterfly's bright wings,
Pretty flowers, trees and songbirds,
So many wondrous things.

Sometimes my gift of beauty's in
A baby's dimpled smile,
Or a kindly word that's given
That makes my day worthwhile.

Bright colored leaves and snowflakes,
A wee kitten, soft and warm,
A rainbow arch across the sky
After a Summer storm.

A bubbly brook in early Spring,
A cardinal in the snow,
The sunset's flame of red and gold
Can set my heart aglow.

So many gifts of beauty
God sends along my day,
And all He asks is that I pause
And look at His display.

Kay Hoffman

Charm and beauty
delight the eye, but
better than either, the
flowers of the field.
Sirach 40:22

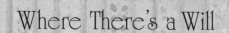
Where There's a Will

Where there's a will, there is a way
To drive your darkest hours away.
Fight on with faith and courage, too,
To bring you hope and strength anew.
Show not the slightest sign of fear,
For someone's always standing near,
And though unseen He still is there
And willing to your burdens share.
One who is always by your side
To be your steadfast Friend and Guide.
That someone who is God above
To fill your heart and soul with love.

Harold F. Mohn

My Prayer for You

I think of you in many ways;
You're always in my prayers.
I ask that God will bless you
And show you how He cares.

I pray that He will hold you
In His everlasting arms,
And ask that He protect you,
And keep you from all harm.

I hope that He will show you
The way to love Him more,
To take your hand and guide you
To Heaven's open door.

I pray that He'll embrace you
And make His will your own.
I hope that He will find you
And take you to His home.

Clara Ashmore

*Then all who take refuge in
You will be glad and forever
shout for joy. Protect them
that You may be the joy of
those who love Your name.*
Psalm 5:12

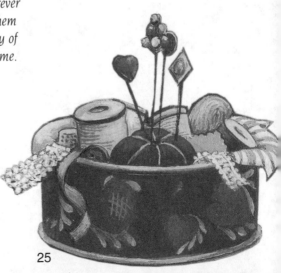

The Wonders of the Lord...

The rain was falling from the skies,
A hard and steady rain –
The heavens opened up and cried,
And washed away my pain...
The rain was falling from the skies,
And glistened on the leaves –
I thought of God and all His love,
And fell down on my knees...
The rain was falling from the skies,
And in my caring heart,
I felt the wonders of the Lord
Of which we are a part!

Hope C. Oberhelman

We Know

We know God makes the sun to shine
And makes the stars to glow.
He cares for every flower and vine,
And makes the river flow.
We know God makes the sky so blue
And makes the raindrops fall.
He touches all the grass with dew –
The Lord, God, makes it all.
We know God makes the birds to sing
And He controls the breeze.
Each season of the year He brings
The lovely, budding trees.
God's wondrous works are everywhere;
Such gifts He does bestow.
He keeps us in His tender care.
God loves the world, we know.

Edna Massimilla

*Thus they will know, as
we know, that there is
no God but You.*
Sirach 36:4

October

When the skies get dark and cloudy,
It is surely going to rain.
When the nights are growing colder,
Then Fall has come again.

It's that lovely season
When leaves turn red and gold,
When though the sun shines brightly,
The days are often cold.

Night now comes so early,
Summer flowers cease to bloom.
Morning fogs drift in the valleys
To create an early morning gloom.

The garden sounds are quiet now,
The birds no longer sing.
Flying high up in the sky,
The geese are on the wing.

The winds of Fall will grow stronger,
The dry leaves will swirl and blow
And snuggle softly on the ground
To wait for Winter's snow.

Milly Patzer

*Guide me in Your truth and teach
me, for You are God my Savior.
For You I wait all the long day,
because of Your goodness, Lord.*
Psalm 25:5

Contemplating

Autumn leaves are falling slowly
Underneath an azure sky,
Dipped in yellow, gold and crimson,
Bidding Summer days good-bye.

Soon in branches, black and barren,
Birds will gather southward bound.
Gone the splendor of the meadows,
Not a flower will be found.

Golden days, so few, so fleeting,
Soon just memories remain.
Winter storms will sweep the meadows,
And the snowbird calls again.

Regina Wiencek

*Between morning and evening
the weather changes; before the
Lord all things are fleeting.*
Sirach 18:26

Autumn Countryside

Warm Summer days are ending,
For autumntime is here.
Tall trees are filigreed in frost,
Wide meadows, brown and sere.

Red sumac by the roadside
Flies banners in the breeze
And golden cobwebs shimmer
Beneath the bare oak trees.

Bright bittersweet burns orange-red,
Blazing over the country lanes,
Where sunsets swirl like rainbows
And God's sparkling stars like silver rain.

Elizabeth Weaver Winstead

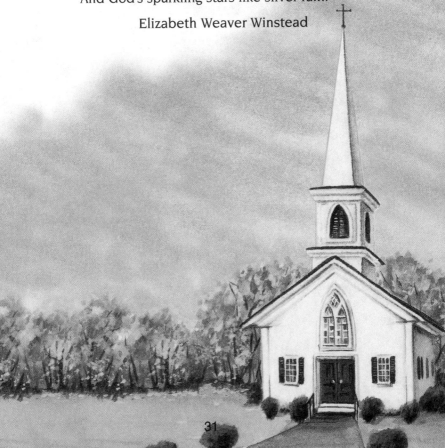

Tomorrow May Be Too Late

Tomorrow may be too late
To tell someone you care,
To utter words you meant to say
When they're no longer there.

Tomorrow may be too late
To visit that old friend
Who shared your life in younger days
You thought would never end.

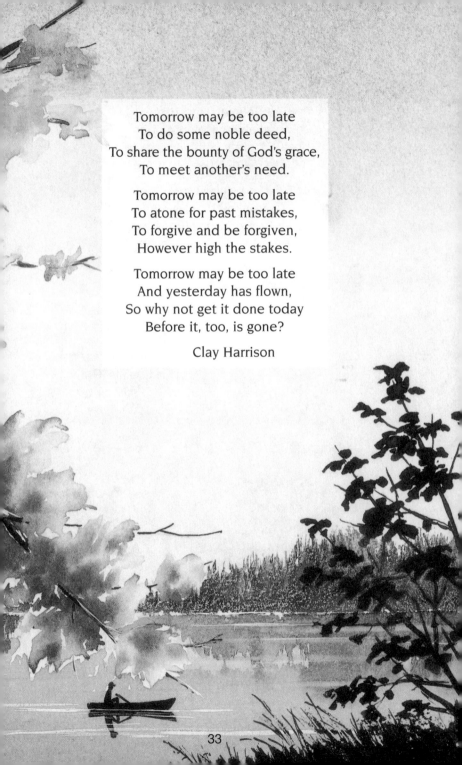

Tomorrow may be too late
To do some noble deed,
To share the bounty of God's grace,
To meet another's need.

Tomorrow may be too late
To atone for past mistakes,
To forgive and be forgiven,
However high the stakes.

Tomorrow may be too late
And yesterday has flown,
So why not get it done today
Before it, too, is gone?

Clay Harrison

Redeeming Song

Abide in Jesus and His word
For receiving Heaven's best.
Jesus invites you in His heart
Where resides peace and rest.

Trust in Jesus who protects
Us from all that's wrong.
Sing Him praises all day long.
Join His redeeming song.

Carol Zileski

Into Your hands I commend
my spirit; You will redeem me,
Lord, faithful God.
Psalm 31:6

I'll Try Again

I thought that I had lost You, God,
Because I failed to do
All I could to earn Your love,
The way I wanted to.

At times I tried so very hard,
But I'd just slip and fall,
And I'll admit that many times
I didn't try at all.

But as I woke this morning,
My faith was very strong,
And suddenly I realized
You've been here all along!

You've never given up on me,
So now I'll try to do
My very best to earn Your love,
And prove my love for You!

Doris A. Orth

*Whatever you ask for in prayer
with faith, you will receive.*
Matthew 21:22

35

Gifts From Our Father

I look around at all the gifts
That God has given me.
Every day brings something new;
His works shine beautifully.

The sunlight on a Winter's day,
The ocean breeze in June,
The beautiful stars that fill the sky,
The golden harvest moon.

All of Nature speaks God's name,
Every creature great and small.
Each one is special in His eyes…
God loves them one and all.

Jill Lemming

Sleep On

Sleep on, oh earth,
Cold winds still sweep the meadows;
The sun forgets to shine days without end.
Sleep on through purple twilight shadows;
On fields and streams rests Winter's icy hand.

Dream on of sunshine and of flowers,
Of birds in flight high in the azure skies,
Of warm wind's soft caress and April showers,
Of soaring kites and children's smiling eyes.

Beneath your ermine cover, sleep,
Until you hear a robin's cheerful song,
And Spring no more plays hide-and-seek,
Until that day, sleep on, sleep on.

Regina Wiencek

In peace I shall both lie down
and sleep, for You alone,
Lord, make me secure.
Psalm 4:9

The River

Life is like a winding river
As it flows out to the sea;
Its journey is not one of ease,
A straight and narrow path not seen,
For its path is full of twists and turns
Like those we find in life,
Some lead to waters calm and still
While others churn with strife.
In the shallows you can walk with ease
And river bottom can be seen.
You're clear of where you're going to,
Every hope and every dream.
But the river can be difficult
And deeper water can be found,
With waters rough and rapid
And its darkness can surround.

In this place upon the river,
We'll not drown, we will survive.
If we keep treading on the river,
Our lives once again will thrive.
For nothing lasts forever
On the river or in life –
Both are filled with many changes,
Cool, still waters, deep, dark strife.
Ever flowing to the sea,
I watch the river move along
And see life's reflection in it
As it sings its river song.

Gina Mazzullo Laurin

*Whoever believes in Me, as scripture
says: "Rivers of living water will
flow from within him."*
John 7:38

Spirit of Peace

One Winter's night as I slept,
I had a dream, and this I dreamt –
The spirit of peace and love
Came in the form of a dove.
As I lay upon my bed
He hovered high above my head.
Quietly, laying very still,
I prayed with all my will,
"Please abide within my heart,
Never let us be far apart.
Come and keep me company,
By God's grace, please enter me."
When I awoke at dawn,
The meaning of my dream took form.
God's heavenly gifts from above
Are earned through prayer and love.
When God is kept in heart and mind,
True love will flow for all mankind.

Jacqui Richardson

There Is Beauty in Store

There is beauty in store,
If it's not for today,
On the mountaintop high,
Up the road just a way.

And not far from my home,
There's a river that winds,
And a small, shady brook
Where the river entwines.

And the countryside's pure,
Seems it's touched from above,
Up the road just a way
And in all of God's love.

And it's great where I go,
If it's but for a day,
For there's beauty in store
Up the road just a way.

Katherine Smith Matheney

*Look up to the skies and
behold; regard the heavens
high above you.*
Job 35:5

41

I Believe

I believe there is a blessing
In store for me each day.
I won't waste the time in seeking it,
For it will surely come my way.
I believe that Spring will follow Winter
No matter how long the wait,
And Nature's beauty will far surpass
Anything that man can make.

I believe that with the rose,
There will always be a thorn.
And with every death that touches us,
A new baby will be born.
I believe the stars continue to shine
When unseen by human eye,
Just as the mountain still is there
While dark clouds are going by.

I believe we all should have
A close fellowship with each other,
And love we have for family
Makes us treat them like a brother.
I believe we all have a special gift
To make life much more sweet
For neighbor, friend, or loved one,
Or whomever we may meet.

I believe God's love was the greatest gift
Given to you and me.
He took our sin upon Himself
And thereby made us free.
Life now has direction since
Salvation I received
From the day I told the Lord,
"By faith I do believe."

Elaine Fowser

Those who trust in Him shall understand truth,
and the faithful shall abide with Him in love:
Because grace and mercy are with His holy ones,
and His care is with the elect.
Wisdom 3:9

Happiness Found

As you use up this day's hours,
Let a smile light up your face,
Wave greetings to a stranger,
Help a loser win the race.

Do a favor for another,
Put some fellow's fear to flight.
You'll be some nearer to Heaven
When you go to bed tonight.

Henry Charles Doherty

A Day at a Time

Why hold so firmly to regrets
And miseries of the past
When unknown pleasures lie ahead,
Endowing us with joy to last?

The past is gone – tomorrow's unknown –
Today's our only gauge
To measure out our slice of joy
As life turns each new page.

Each day's a blank page of our life,
A page that we should fill
With golden deeds and loving thoughts
Designed to do His will.

So don't hold on to yesterdays,
Old sins and ills to nurture,
For filling now with useless past
Will not leave room for future.

Shirley Takacs

Fill us at daybreak with Your love,
that all our days we may sing for joy.
Psalm 90:14

Amazing Graces

One knows our Lord is still alive,
Just look around and see
The beauty of this earth we know
In its entirety.
He never ceases to show His love
In all the flowers that bloom,
In loveliness we can behold
The stars and silver moon.
We thank You, Lord, for lovely days,
The warmth upon our faces,
And flowers blooming everywhere
In such amazing graces.

Katherine Smith Matheney

God's Miracles

The snow creeps back beneath the shrubs
Then disappears from there,
And flowers bud and bloom – ah yes,
Sweet fragrance fills the air.

The sunlight glints from melting ice,
Where there is a touch of green,
While Nature with resurgent life
Paints such a lovely scene.

Forsythia and crocus bloom
And robins on the wing –
God's miracles again refresh
The earth. Ah yes, 'tis Spring!

Luther Elvis Albright

... birds of Heaven nest;
among the branches they sing.
Psalm 104:12

A Springtime Harvest

Folks often think a harvest
Occurs in Autumn each year,
But if we look real closely,
Spring yields a harvest dear.

There's the harvest of the blossoms,
Such as a flowering dogwood tree,
Apples ripening in the orchard
And gardens welcoming each seed.

Showers bring on a harvest of colors,
Such as a rainbow's vibrant hue,
Newborn colts will try to stand
And calves will cry out "moo!"

Violets, azaleas, and daffodils,
Sprinkled by the morning dew,
The harvest seems unending
And there's so much to see and do!

So quickly gather the springtime harvest
And give God thanks for this gift of love,
But don't forget Autumn's soon approaching
With another abundant harvest from above.

Linda C. Grazulis

Our Earthly Garden

Acres of sunflowers,
Gardens of roses,
The song of creation
Which God composes.
The morning glories are
Climbing the fences.
With the hand of God,
The garden enhances.

Be it Spring or Summer
Or the beauty of Fall,
Living the seasons
Is Nature's call.
And Winter, too,
The snow surrounds,
With living sculptures
In silver-white gowns.

James Joseph Huesgen

You will show me the path to life,
abounding in Your presence, the delights
at Your right hand forever.
Psalm 16:11

Caring Arms

In the caring arms of Jesus,
There is peace of heart and mind
And the guidance of His wisdom
For each soul of humankind;
There is a balm for all our heartaches
And a haven for despair
When we trust Him as our Savior
And we worship Him in prayer.

There is healing for our bruises
And a love that is sublime –
With compassion and forgiveness
For transgressions of our time;
Every day is a day of glory
In the arms of His embrace
When our heart is in His keeping
And our soul is in His grace.

Michael Dubina

The Lord is my strength and my
shield, in whom my heart trusted and
found help. So my heart rejoices;
with my song I praise God.
Psalm 28:7

Nature Plays

The winds of change blow softly
As Winter turns to Spring.
Sunlight gentle on the earth
Brings life to everything.

Birds sing sweetly in a tree,
Building their new nest.
A rabbit dares to venture out,
Curious like the rest.

Clouds are forming pictures
Way up in the sky,
Flowers opening their petals,
Brilliant color to the eye.

Faces wearing smiles,
Hearts are full of hope,
Children laughing near the pond,
Swinging from a rope.

Leaves swirling on the grass,
With each new breeze that blows,
They start dancing in a circle –
'Round and 'round they go.

God looks down upon us
In His tender, loving way
And, pleased with this creation,
Watches Nature play.

Marge Ramsey

Sing to the Lord a new song;
sing to the Lord, all the earth.
Psalm 96:1

The Gift of Time

We enter the dawn of each new year;
Equal time is our gift to spend,
So what we achieve with our portion
Makes all the difference in the end.

Time once spent can't be recalled.
There is only one chance to use it.
This gift is more precious than gold;
We should take care not to lose it!

Time passes swift as an eagle,
Winging high in the heavens above.
Love can be shared in a moment;
All the world really needs is love!

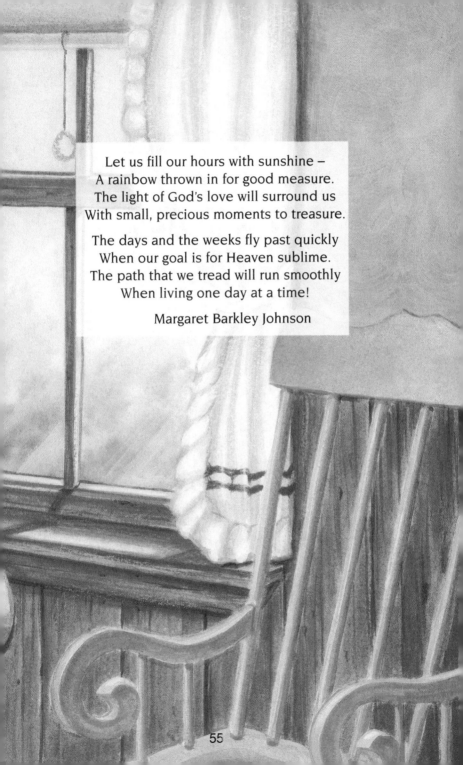

Let us fill our hours with sunshine –
A rainbow thrown in for good measure.
The light of God's love will surround us
With small, precious moments to treasure.

The days and the weeks fly past quickly
When our goal is for Heaven sublime.
The path that we tread will run smoothly
When living one day at a time!

Margaret Barkley Johnson

Bridges of Faith

I am building a bridge,
Comprised of faith and love,
Across the great crevasse
From my heart to God above.

The beams are slowly constructed
Of belief in His words,
Captured from the Bible page
To which my eyes are lured.

I'll have a strong foundation
From that which I have learned
To build a sturdy base
And a life for all concerned.

Rebecca Sweeney

We Are Blessed

The world and all that's in it
Is a gift from God, you see.
All the wonderment and beauty
Was created for you and me.

How precious is our Savior
To share His gifts this way.
We are reminded of His love for us
By the things we see each day.

If at times we're filled with sorrow
And should happen to be depressed,
Just see God's miracles around us
And know that we are blessed.

When skies are bright and sunny,
Dwell on the splendor that God shares
And let's not forget to thank Him
When we go to Him in prayer.

Shirley Hile Powell

*Blessed be God, who did not refuse me
the kindness I sought in prayer.*
Psalm 66:20

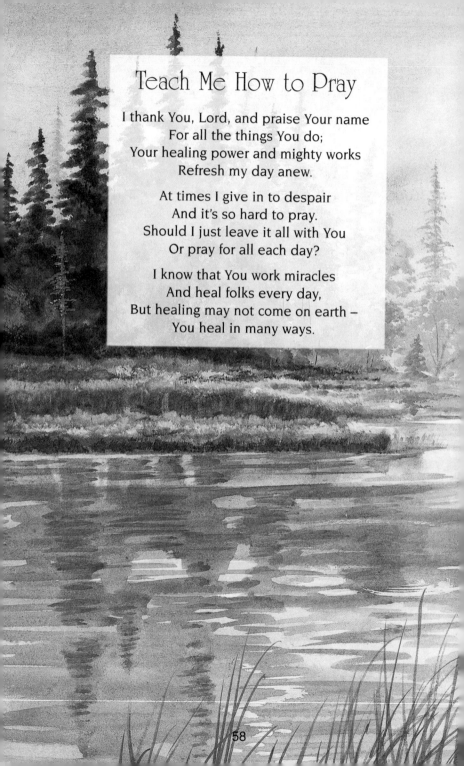

Teach Me How to Pray

I thank You, Lord, and praise Your name
For all the things You do;
Your healing power and mighty works
Refresh my day anew.

At times I give in to despair
And it's so hard to pray.
Should I just leave it all with You
Or pray for all each day?

I know that You work miracles
And heal folks every day,
But healing may not come on earth –
You heal in many ways.

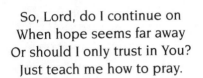

So, Lord, do I continue on
When hope seems far away
Or should I only trust in You?
Just teach me how to pray.

"Thy will be done" should always be
The center of each prayer
And when I kneel before Your throne,
Lord, You are always there.

I thank You, Lord, and praise Your name
For blessings every day.
Just lead me as I seek Your will –
Lord, teach me how to pray.

Gertrude B. McClain

Walk With God Each Day

God's eye is on the sparrow,
He hears the fishes cry,
His compassionate mercy
Falls on you and I.
He who holds the universe
Takes note of falling tears.
When we open wide our hearts,
He walks us through the years.
The Lord is near the broken-hearted,
Crushed spirits feel renewed
When we keep God in our presence,
Always in our view.
Although we might grieve at times
When sorrow comes our way,
We find life worth living
When we walk with God each day.

Jacqui Richardson

Awareness

Lord, make me aware of each blessing,
The ones that I miss every day,
Like skies that are blue and flowers in bloom
And friends that I meet on my way.

When my negative thoughts are too many
And only the dark clouds I see,
Remind me, O Lord, of Your presence
In this day You have given to me.

Even when stillness surrounds me
And thoughts are the company I keep,
Let Your word and Your spirit be with me,
Bringing comfort and peace to my sleep.

And tomorrow when cares would confront me,
I will take a few moments to rest
And look at the sky and the flowers
And think of the ways I am blessed.

Judy Schwab

*May the God of hope fill you with
all the joy and peace in believing,
so that you may abound in hope
by the power of the Holy Spirit.*
Romans 15:13

Sand Prints

Our lives are footprints in the sand
Which the waves of time erase;
Deep or shallow fare the same –
All gone without a trace.

In youth we tread on aimless feet
With little thought or care
That those who follow in our steps
May find the surface bare.

In later years the pace has slowed;
With backward glance we see
The prints are quickly fading
And soon will cease to be.

So cherish moments in the sun,
Give thanks for every day,
For no one can be certain when
Their trail may wash away.

Mortal tracks upon the sand
Were never meant to last,
But eternal is the mark of God
Where we have merely passed.

C. David Hay

God's teaching is in their hearts;
their steps do not falter.
Psalm 37:31

Home Is

Home is such a lovely place,
A gentle touch – a smiling face,
The laughter of a happy child,
A quietness – a heart beguiled,
Togetherness at each day's end,
A miracle that life can lend.
Home is happiness supreme,
It's caring minds that share a dream,
A reaching lawn – a climbing tree,
A new tomorrow yet to be,
It's Mom and Dad and blessings true,
Believing in a dream come true.
The simple joys we find each day,
A time for work – a time for play,
It's warmth and peace, yet so much more,
It's all our hearts are searching for,
A trusting faith in God above,
But all that's best for home is love.

Garnett Ann Schultz

Sweet Release

The time has come, oh blessed Lord,
To thank Thee for Thy grace
And bless Thee for Thy precious hope
And Thy tender, warm embrace...

The time has come, oh blessed Lord,
To take away my pain,
And fill my life with happiness
And sunshine after rain...

The time has come, oh blessed Lord,
To look to Thee for love,
And reach for happiness and joy
And blessings from above...

The time has come, oh blessed Lord,
To ask Thee for Thy peace,
And in the quiet of the night
To find Thy sweet release...

Hope C. Oberhelman

*Hallelujah! How good to
celebrate our God in song; how
sweet to give fitting praise.
Psalm 147:1*

Take the Time

Did you take time out today
To offer thanks to God and pray,
And thank Him for His gifts of love,
Bestowed on you from Heaven above?

It is the least that you can do
For all the blessings given you.
So set aside some time each day
And humbly kneel to God and pray.

Harold F. Mohn

God Gives Me

God gives me the strength and courage;
He provides for all my needs.
I can walk with Him in glory;
All my efforts will succeed.

God gives me the light and wisdom,
Guiding me through every day.
My decisions all are destined;
By His will, I shall not stray.

God gives me encouragement
To forge ahead with reverence.
I cannot fail, for He restores
My faith, my hope, my confidence.

God gives me His love and mercy;
He upholds me tenderly.
I cannot fail, nor foster fear
With the blessings God gives me.

Patience Allison Hartbauer

*Hallelujah! Give thanks to
the Lord, who is good, whose
love endures forever.*
Psalm 106:1

May the God of hope fill you with all joy and peace in believing, so that you may abound in hope by the power of the Holy Spirit.

Romans 15:13

A Day to Remember

This heart of mine will ever see
This green wood where the trees
All whisper in October's sun
To every passing breeze.

Where evergreens in majesty
Sweep Heaven with their crowns,
While thistles and wildflowers wear
Their starry Autumn gowns.

The gentle cool, the fiery Fall,
The valley filled with peace,
The singing birds, the dancing stream,
The southbound flight of geese.

They fill my heart, they lift my soul,
They make my life worthwhile,
The sun – God's love, the wind – His kiss,
My happiness – His smile!

Kate Watkins Furman

Autumn Moods

Autumn raises its sleepy head
In tones of yellow, orange and red.
With moods, it brings here to the fore
With Winter knocking at our door.
I see mornings white where frost has been.
In the wind, small saplings will careen.
And the leaves are blowing to the ground
With just a hush… a shuffling sound,
As if the earth is changing now
And Summer leaves with one last bow.
Then the earth turns white with snow
And whistling songs as harsh winds blow.
To feel the moods the season brings
Recalls to me so many things.
Hues disappear with the rusting sod,
Here… the ever-present hand of God.

James Joseph Huesgen

Life

We meet with smiles, meet with tears
Along the trail of life;
Sometimes the days are sunny
And then come days of strife.

But there can be no rainbows
Without the drops of rain,
And there can be no healing
Without the pangs of pain.

In Nature there's a balance,
God planned it just that way,
And so it is with us, friends,
We've bright and strife-filled days.

So, absorb the rays of sunshine
While on the trail of life,
And God will give us courage
When come the days of strife.

Loise Pinkerton Fritz

*And not only so, but we glory in
tribulations also: knowing that
tribulation worketh patience;
and patience, experience; and
experience, hope...*
Romans 5:3,4

The Voice Within

There's a voice that lives within my heart
And talks to me each day
And helps me guide my wayward steps
Along life's treacherous way.
It speaks to me of virtues
And whispers words of hope.
It keeps my flagging spirits high
When I have failed to cope.

This voice beguiles my very soul
And stills the demons there.
It makes me know that in this world
There's worlds of love to share.
And I know peace in turmoil's midst,
Strength beyond my own,
Joy too great to put in words,
For I know I'm not alone.

If you but listen to your heart,
You'll hear this voice I share,
For it speaks not to me alone,
It's there for all who care.
And the dawning of a brave new age
Is waiting to begin
When each of us can hear and heed
That little voice within.

Bill Hazel

With God

Remember me and strengthen me
If only this one time;
Help to end my struggle,
Lift up this soul of mine.
Enlighten me and guide me,
If only for one hour;
Aid me in my troubles,
Show my soul Your power.
Love me and protect me
In Your hallowed way.
Until this life is over,
With You my soul will stay.

Rebecca Sweeney

Life's Road

Today I stand beside the road,
Bowed down beneath life's heavy load;
Then as I view the trail ahead,
My mind, my heart, are filled with dread,
For who can say what lies beyond
That hill, that curve, that placid pond?
Will I know heartache, toil and tears,
Or will I laugh away the years?
Or will I feel pain within my frame,
Or rise to fortune, power and fame?
I sigh and start to travel on
When suddenly, I'm not alone,
For there beside me walks a Friend,
A Friend on whom I can depend
To lead me on whate'er betide;
I smile, then follow Him – my Guide.

Chris Ahlemann

*Guide me in Your truth and teach
me, for You are God my Savior. For
You I wait all the long day, because
of Your goodness, Lord.*
Psalm 25:5

Storm Clouds

There are days when you have felt
That life has passed you by.
Instead of sunshine in your life,
Dark storm clouds fill your sky.
But remember that all storms must pass
And beyond the clouds above,
There in the heavens our Lord dwells
And shines down on us with love.

Dolores Karides

He Hung the Moon

He hung the moon and the stars in the skies.
To see all His wonders, He gave us our eyes.
He made flowers and trees, the winds and the breeze
And fashioned our bodies to enjoy all of these.

Such beautiful melodies sound in our ears;
He fashioned our bodies so these we could hear.
To hear and to see and to feel and to touch,
Of blessings and joys, He gave us so much.

Though we search to discover as years come and go,
Yet all His great wonders we never can know.
So great yet He stoops to the heart of each man
To reveal His eternal salvation plan.

How wonderfully made are we, body and soul;
He added His spirit so we would be whole.
Our God is so great, so wise, so divine,
Yet He wishes to dwell in your heart and mine.

Helen Gleason

*How great are His signs, how mighty His
wonders; His kingdom is an everlasting
kingdom, and His dominion endures
through all generations.*
Daniel 3:100

Praise Him

Praise Him in the morning
When the dawn is breaking,
As the quiet settles,
O'er the day's awakening.

Praise Him in the noontime
When from work you're resting.
Thank Him for His gracious love
And strength in time of testing.

Praise Him in the twilight
When the sun is sinking,
And there comes contentment
With a time for thinking.

Praise Him in the nighttime,
Tho' some fears are mounting.
Just keep praising Jesus
While your blessings counting.

Praise Him for His guidance
Through the day that's ending.
Praise Him for the morrow,
Safe within His tending.

Praise Him! Ever praise Him!
Praise Him with thanksgiving.
Praise Him for His goodness
Through each day of living!

Beverly J. Anderson

Seasons of Life

Our lives have many seasons
And we all must realize…
That one day we'll have sunshine
And the next, comes gloomy skies.

It's all a part of living
In the place we now reside…
But in truth, it's only temporal –
For in Heaven we'll abide.

So when the dark clouds hover
And you think they will not flee…
Just remember, Heaven's waiting
Where the sun will shine for thee.

Jill Lemming

Within His Grandeur

Soft clouds drop low to touch the hills
As if they wish to hide.
Intrusive peaks dressed white by snow,
Which through the Winter bide
Their time, until a warming sun
Shall push the chill away
And beam the clouds to cirriform
Above the April day.

And once again the blue divides
The heavens from below,
And mountains rise to majesties
That only they can know.
At home am I in this domain
Within the grandeur of
These sights that only God can give
As tokens of His love.

Henry W. Gurley

Love Is the Answer

Once I was feeling so worthless –
Unsure of just where I fit in.
Then You came to me, my precious Lord,
And restored my faith once again.

You knew I was troubled,
So You took my hand
And spoke to me softly,
So I'd understand…

That our worth isn't measured
By wealth or by fame,
But by all the love we give
To others, Lord, in Your name.

We could start with just a smile –
Perhaps a gentle touch,
Or the all important hug
That means so very much.

So I no longer feel worthless;
I have so much love to give.
You filled my heart with more than enough
To last me as long as I live!

Doris A. Orth

*Answer me, Lord, in Your
generous love; in Your great
mercy turn to me.*
Psalm 69:17

Proclaim the greatness of His name, loudly sing His praises, with music on the harp and all stringed instruments; sing out with joy as you proclaim.

Sirach 39:15

The Music of Life

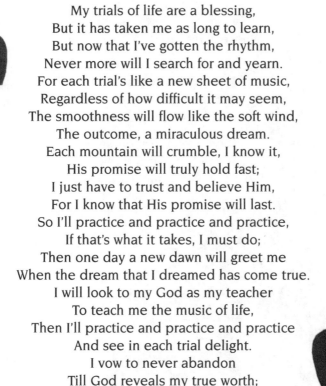

My trials of life are a blessing,
But it has taken me as long to learn,
But now that I've gotten the rhythm,
Never more will I search for and yearn.
For each trial's like a new sheet of music,
Regardless of how difficult it may seem,
The smoothness will flow like the soft wind,
The outcome, a miraculous dream.
Each mountain will crumble, I know it,
His promise will truly hold fast;
I just have to trust and believe Him,
For I know that His promise will last.
So I'll practice and practice and practice,
If that's what it takes, I must do;
Then one day a new dawn will greet me
When the dream that I dreamed has come true.
I will look to my God as my teacher
To teach me the music of life,
Then I'll practice and practice and practice
And see in each trial delight.
I vow to never abandon
Till God reveals my true worth;
I will then rejoice in the splendor
For the music I learned here on earth.

Chris Zambernard

Sing praise, play music; proclaim
all His wondrous deeds!
Psalm 105:2

Only a Moment

It only takes a moment
To give a word of cheer,
To warm the heart of someone
Whose skies are dark and drear.

It only takes a moment
To clasp another's hand,
Tell him that you'd like to help,
You care and understand.

It only takes a moment,
And yet, in hurried pace,
We oft neglect small kindnesses,
A frown upon our face.

Perhaps we have forgotten
When in our hour of need
How much it meant when others gave
A kindly word or deed.

It only takes a moment
To breathe a little prayer,
Asking God to bless His children
In places everywhere.

These precious little moments
Send winging far and near,
Like homing pigeons that will return
To bring our own heart cheer.

Kay Hoffman

Passing Moments

Lord, at the end of this day,
May we look back without regret.
During the minutes and hours,
May we never forget
To make life more pleasant
For every person we meet –
Friends and neighbors,
People in the street –
Putting into practice
The words we believe,
Be more willing to give
Rather than to receive,
To always be cheerful
In others' sight,
Filled with courage
From morning till night,
Be more thoughtful
In all that we do.
Each day may we grow
Just a little like You.

Jacqui Richardson

The Presence of God

I see God in the rainbow
That arcs across the sky;
The lovely shining colors
Remind me God is nigh.

I see Him in the season,
The greening of the Spring,
In all the vivid flowers
That April showers bring.

I hear Him in the laughter
Of children when they play;
Their innocence an echo
When I kneel down to pray.

I feel God in the silence
When evening shadows creep;
My soul records His presence
When I drift off to sleep.

Delphine LeDoux

*Enter, let us bow down in
worship; let us kneel before
the Lord who made us.*
Psalm 95:6

How Blessed

How blessed are the morning hours
Before daily chores begin,
To spend some private time with God,
To praise and worship Him,
To lift concerns that are on your heart
And leave them in His care,
To know prayers are responded to
Before you leave them there.

How blessed is that quiet time
When you and God commune;
Knowing that He cares for you
Lifts up the darkest gloom.
All your cares and troubled woes
Are transformed into peace;
How blessed is that moment when
All hurt and trouble cease.
How blessed is your time with Him
When you take the time to pray;
It gives you joy, it gives you strength
That lasts throughout the day.

Nancy Watson Dodrill

Blessed be God, who did
not refuse me the kindess
I sought in prayer.
Psalm 66:20

Serene Spring

I gaze upon the meadow
With a feeling so serene,
Soaking up the beauty
Of the lush fields of green.

A very tranquil moment
Seems to hold me in its spell,
Leaves me with a feeling
That all is going well.

The woods are lined with redbuds
Mixed with silver green.
Clouds cast their shadows
Where the splintered branches lean.

Wildflowers scattered carefully
Throughout the rolling hills,
Giving bees their nectar,
A fulfillment of God's will.

Shirley Hile Powell

A Special Day

Savor the moments of today –
The smells, the sights and the sounds.
Make it the day of yesterday's dream,
When your hopes and wishes are found.

Rise with the sun and thrill to its light.
Smell the honeysuckle in the morning dew.
Listen to the birds and the song they sing.
Feel each kiss as the wind blows through.

Look for the happiness you deserve.
Find the positive when things go wrong.
Treasure each hour as it ticks away
Because in a blink, it's forever gone.

Remember today is soon part of the past,
Gone like a feather that floats in the breeze.
And as time passes by, you say to yourself,
"I made today special, and for that I am pleased."

Gloria Swan Kennedy

May Your kindness, Lord,
be upon us; we have put
our hope in You.
Psalm 33:22

God's Majesty

As I walk through the fields so free,
My thoughts run deep inside of me.
I stop and lay on the grass I tread,
I prop my arms beneath my head,
I close my eyes and breathe in deep,
I put my soul into His keep,
I smell the air so clean, so pure,
I feel the wind and then I'm sure.
Opening slowly my eyes so still,
I look to Heaven – my soul does fill.
The clouds float by, the sun shines bright,
That's when you sense His awesome might.
Tho' clouds conceal the shining sun,
Its rays pass over and we are one.
It's then I know and truly feel
That God is good and very real.

Billy Parker

I Thank Thee

I thank Thee, Lord, for sunny days
And for the rain that comes our way,
For skies of blue, a morn that's new,
A friend who kneels with me to pray.

I thank Thee, Lord, for things that grow,
For cooling winds that gently blow,
For harvest's reaping food to eat,
For shady trees in the Summer heat…

For flowers that cheer with colors gay,
Delighting eyes along life's way,
For mountain high, the ocean's sway,
For glorious sunset's end of day…

For Nature's treasures made for us,
A heart to love, Your word to trust,
For ears to hear and eyes to see,
But I thank Thee most that You love me.

Helen Gleason

*We thank You, God, we give
thanks; we call upon Your name,
declare Your wonderful deeds.*
Psalm 75:2

95

Look to Your Heart

If you feel you have nothing
Of value to give
In this meaningless portion
Of life that you live…

Don't surrender your spirit
Because if you do,
You'll forfeit contentment
Allotted to you…

Contentment that comes
When you know at the start
You've distinguished yourself
As you give of the heart.

Some sad soul is waiting
For someone like you
To brighten his day
Through a kind deed or two.

It need cost you nothing
In dollars and cents,
Yet think of the rare gift
You'll humbly present.

And only God knows
The graces you'll gain,
While a deep sense of giving
In your heart shall remain.

Catherine Janssen Irwin

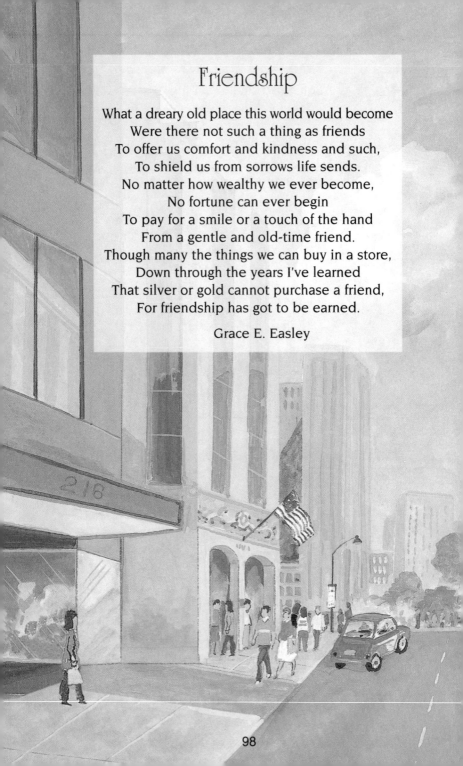

Friendship

What a dreary old place this world would become
Were there not such a thing as friends
To offer us comfort and kindness and such,
To shield us from sorrows life sends.
No matter how wealthy we ever become,
No fortune can ever begin
To pay for a smile or a touch of the hand
From a gentle and old-time friend.
Though many the things we can buy in a store,
Down through the years I've learned
That silver or gold cannot purchase a friend,
For friendship has got to be earned.

Grace E. Easley

The Highway Known as Life

We're walking down the highway,
The highway known as life;
As we tread this highway,
We'll meet with joy, some strife.

Oft times there will be detours,
Some "stop's" and then some "go's;"
We'll pass through happy valleys,
Sometimes crawl mountain roads.

If all our days were sunshine,
Our tendency might be
To lose sight of our Savior
And wander aimlessly.

So as we walk life's highway,
See dark and sunny days,
Remember there's a reason…
God's strengthening our faith.

Loise Pinkerton Fritz

*The Lord is good, a strong hold in
the day of trouble; and He knoweth
them that trust in Him.
Nahum 1:7*

Peaceful Reflection

Think today where'er you wander,
Think of all the good you've done,
Think today and as you ponder,
Watch the setting of the sun.

See the dark turn into evening,
Peaceful shadows all around you.
Now's the time for firm believing,
As these miracles confound you.

Miracles like life and laughter,
Tide of ocean, depth of sea.
Miracles that, ever after,
Will be there for you, for me.

Close your eyes in peaceful sleep now.
Worry not about tomorrow.
Yesterday is gone, don't weep now,
Save the joy and leave the sorrow.

Breaks the dawn, a new beginning.
Take it! Make it! Never fear!
Here's your chance, your time for winning,
For a new day's drawing near.

Jeanne Emory Douglas

*Reflect on what I am saying,
for the Lord will give you
understanding in everything.*
2 Timothy 2:7

A Cup of Tea and Tenderness

A cup of tea and tenderness
Can lift a weary soul
When words are at a loss to help
And life has taken its toll.

To rest awhile and share a sip,
For it doesn't cost a cent
To chat about some good times
And become a bit unbent.

Worries seem to diminish
As the kettle dips and pours.
Hearts become much warmer
As one cup leads to more.

Soon laughter will fill the room
And tenderness abound.
God created friends and tea
As a pick-up when one's down.

Linda C. Grazulis

You Reveal Your Love

You reveal Your love
In such gentle things –
In a baby's smile,
In each bird that sings,
In the Summer breeze,
In a wide-eyed fawn,
In a mother's love,
In the blush of dawn.

You reveal Your love
In such quiet things –
In each flower that blooms,
In the peace prayer brings,
In the sunset's glow,
In the stars above.
In the hills and trees,
You reveal Your love.

Gentle, quiet things
Bringing peace to me –
Tokens of Your love
And Your majesty;
Lord, I thank You so
With a heart of praise
For Your love revealed
In such special ways.

Beverly J. Anderson

*The Lord is my strength and my
shield, in whom my heart trusted and
found help. So my heart rejoices; with
my song I praise my God.*
Psalm 28:7

What Lies in Our Hearts

What lies in our hearts
Reflects in the way
That we live our lives
On this earth day to day.

When we live for God
Our hearts are love-filled.
Peace, hope, and joy
Are deeply instilled.

Happiness is shown
Through the smiles on our face
As we cope with the problems
Of life's daily race.

When we help others
In their time of need,
We are pleasing our Savior,
Who sees our kind deed.

May we always be willing
To share a small part
Of the goodness and kindness
That lies in our hearts.

Shirley Hile Powell

*May He grant you joy of
heart and may peace
abide among you.*
Sirach 50:23

To Greet the Day

Greet each day with gladness;
Awake and rub your eyes.
Look upon the morning
As the sun begins to rise.

Shake hands with a brand-new morning;
Yesterday has had its farewell...
Drink in the beauty of today
As it casts its magic spell.

Give thanks for this new awakening,
As birds sing melodies rare...
Can any music of the spheres
Ever quite compare?

There's hope for another tomorrow,
Sparkling fresh with morning dew,
But quickly is gone with the fading of dawn
As daylight comes into view.

So, don't waste another morning
Without rising to greet the day,
For like the dawn you may soon be gone
And let this blessing slip away.

Lou Ella Cullipher

Only goodness and love will pursue me all
the days of my life; I will dwell in the
house of the Lord for years to come.

Psalm 23:6

God Understands

God understands your sorrow,
He hears the smallest prayers,
So give Him all your problems –
He understands and He cares.

No matter what the need is,
It may be large or small,
God is never in a hurry –
He listens to them all.

So put your trust in Jesus,
He is your dearest Friend;
Don't worry about the future –
He is with you to the end.

Helen Ruth Ashton

Use Me, Lord

Use me, Lord, to strengthen those
Who need a helping hand.
Give me the words to comfort those
Who are struggling to understand.

May I lay aside my grief,
Help those who cannot cope,
And let me represent the One
Who came to give us hope!

When human frailties weigh me down,
So low I cannot stand,
'Til then, I pray, show me the way
To serve my fellow man.

Mary S. Chevalier

*I will instruct you and show
you the way you should
walk, give you counsel and
watch over you.*
Psalm 32:8

Thanks Be to God for Friendship

Thanks be to God for faithful friends
Who bless my life each day,
Those who come before I call
To chase my blues away.

Thanks be to God for friendships
That last throughout the years,
For those who hug the hurts away
And wipe away my tears.

How precious are the memories
That only friends can share,
The secrets kept in confidence
And joys of answered prayer.

How sweet the sound of laughter
That fills an empty room,
Those sweet, familiar voices
And smiles that always bloom.

How sweet the thoughts that linger
When friends are far away...
Thanks be to God for faithful friends
Who bless my life each day!

Clay Harrison

*Sing praise to the Lord,
you faithful; give thanks
to God's holy name.*
Psalm 30:5

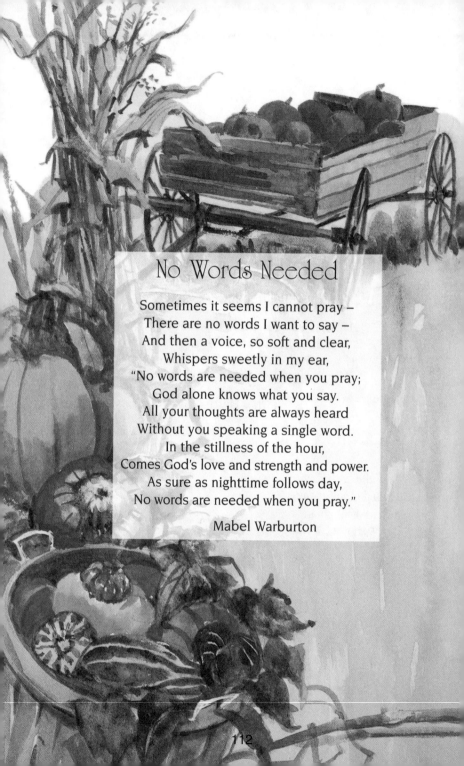

No Words Needed

Sometimes it seems I cannot pray –
There are no words I want to say –
And then a voice, so soft and clear,
Whispers sweetly in my ear,
"No words are needed when you pray;
God alone knows what you say.
All your thoughts are always heard
Without you speaking a single word.
In the stillness of the hour,
Comes God's love and strength and power.
As sure as nighttime follows day,
No words are needed when you pray."

Mabel Warburton

Harvest Thanks

Each season yields its gifts sublime,
But none quite like the autumntime.
Sweet, tangy smell of orchards ripe
Can't help but bring the heart delight.

The country mart now overflows
With bounty that God's hand bestows.
Vegetables, fruits and grain heaped high,
Fat pumpkins for a special pie.

The garden patch is bedded down,
Chestnuts are carpeting the ground.
The cider's cooling, sweet as wine,
Lush grapes are purpling on the vine.

Come, let us thank our caring God
Who gives the seed, the fertile sod,
Who sends the rain, the sun to shine
And once again, the harvest time.

Kay Hoffman

*For then you shall delight in the
Almighty and you shall lift up
your face toward God.*
Job 22:26

Multicolored Autumn Days

Autumn leaves are falling now,
Carpeting the ground
Like pieces of a puzzle
Waiting to be found.

The clear, blue skies of summertime
Are slowly turning gray,
As farmers reap their harvests
With gratitude each day.

There is frost on the pumpkins now
In fields mile after mile,
But soon they will beguile us
With jack-o'-lantern smiles.

There's cider at every roadside stand
And candied apples, too,
With gourds in assorted sizes
And mums of every hue.

As multicolored Autumn days
Unravel near and far,
Each one serves to remind us
How richly blessed we are!

Clay Harrison

Loving Life

I can't help loving life
Because it's such a precious gift;
Just looking all about me,
I get a sudden lift.
The world is packed with everything
To please the eyes and mind,
And the colors of the seasons
Are the very brightest kind.

The path that lies before me,
God placed with loving care;
It's wide enough so we can walk
Together, everywhere.
It doesn't really matter
If the shadows hide the sun,
For loving life, and loving God,
Is what I've always done.

Grace E. Easley

God's Presence

If we would just take a moment
Out of every busy day
To reflect and contemplate on God
And go to Him and pray,
Then God in all His goodness
Will transcend His love to us
And life would be much smoother
With very little fuss.
He is always there to guide us
If we do His holy will.
He will protect and guard us,
For He is love fulfilled.
He gave us each an angel
To help in times of need;
They are His holy messengers
And their warnings we must heed.
So off and on throughout the day,
Let us go to Him in prayer,
And as we quietly call on Him,
We will feel His presence there.

Shirley Hile Powell

Only goodness and love will
pursue me all the days of my
life; I will dwell in the house of
the Lord for years to come.
Psalm 23:6

117

Earthly Wealth

We are told to treat others
As we'd like them to treat us,
Dispel the negative thoughts,
To avoid any fuss.

The cockles of one's heart warm
When sharing love and care.
It makes one happy, feeling
God put us here to share.

Do not look for a reward –
It's now, within your heart.
You feel the satisfaction
Of having done your part.

Thank God for this chance to serve,
For being His steward.
You're living His precious word,
Which is your best reward.

To think of others in need,
Forgetting 'bout yourself,
Brings the blessings of God's love –
This is your earthly wealth!

Mary Conn

*For the Lord's work is true;
all His works are trustworthy.*
Psalm 33:4

My Prayer for Those in Need

Oh, Lord, for every neighbor, kin or friend
To whom I've said, "I'll pray for you today,"
For those who have a broken heart to mend
Or find their lives in total disarray…
For all who hurt in body, soul or mind,
Today I offer every thought and deed.
Each time I'm giving, gracious, good or kind,
Please share, oh God, Your grace with those in need.
May all my works and everything I do,
My every joy and pain, each prayer I say,
Reflect the caring goodness shown by You
And help my friends for whom I pray today.

Polly Thornton

Before We Top the Hill

In this world there's tribulation
As we travel on our way;
The skies aren't always sunny,
Sometimes they turn to gray.
For man's born unto trouble
As upward fly the sparks,
But we need never worry,
For God is standing guard.

"I have overcome the world,"
Christ said, "Be of good cheer."
Then let us fully trust in Him,
He'll dry our every tear.
When tribulation comes our way,
As in this world it will,
Remember it's a valley trod
Before we top the hill.

Loise Pinkerton Fritz

Yet man is born unto trouble,
as the sparks fly upward.
Job 5:7

121

You're Seeing Him

When you gaze at the stars
All twinkling and bright,
When you see the snow sparkle
From moonbeams at night…

When you watch the sun rise
With the new morning light,
Or a bird's caught your eye
As it soars freely in flight…

Our Lord gives us these
To show us a part
Of Himself and the beauty
That's deep in His heart.

They're each such a blessing
For us to behold,
More precious than diamonds,
More costly than gold.

They fill us with wonder,
With awe and delight,
As we gaze at the beauty
Of each wondrous sight.

So whether you're watching
The sun slowly set
Or you're gazing at flowers
In bloom, don't forget...

You're seeing Him.

Gina Laurin

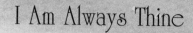

I Am Always Thine

I will not fear the future,
Nor what's in store for me;
God's love will lead and guide me
Through all eternity.

His love is ever constant
And He takes care of me.
He fills my life with blessings;
No harm can come to me.

With faith and hope deep in my heart,
Then peace and joy are mine.
Dear Lord, You're always with me
And I am always Thine.

Dolores Karides

The Here and Now

Our days are busy, weeks so full,
We scarce can savor God's own peace,
To bask in all the beauty 'round us,
Feeling joy while troubles cease.

Look off to hills of rolling green
That yearn to stretch and touch the sky;
Elusive blue beyond the reach
Of jagged mountains thrusting high.

Or trees and buds; yes, snow and ice –
All wondrous parts of His great plan.
Tomorrow's joy is made today!
Enjoy the moment while we can.

And live the present; hear His word.
Whatever's past is out of sight.
This precious season, ours today!
Behold the world! Let in His light!

Helen M. Motti

*Learn to savor how good the
Lord is; happy are those who
take refuge in Him.*
Psalm 34:9

Whatever you ask for in prayer with
faith, you will receive.
Matthew 21:22

The Quilt of Life

Each day is fresh, new material,
An opportunity to design
Today's pattern, in the quilt of life.
May what I create be true and fine.

Heavenly Father, guide my hand.
Help each part be cut with care
According to Your pattern planned,
Sewn with faith, fine-stitched with prayer.

Though I may quilt no masterpiece,
Let my product be humbly done,
A warm, enduring gift of love –
A tribute to Your precious Son!

Louise Pugh Corder

*Majestic and glorious is
Your work, Your wise
design endures forever.
Psalm 111:3*

The Simplest of Things

A smile, a touch, a kind, healing word,
A gesture to show that you care,
Surely the simplest of things are the best,
When daily with others you share.

It may be just listening or giving your time
To someone who's feeling alone,
And even your silence when given in love
Is worth every word on its own.

Surely the things we yearn for the most
Are the things we also should give.
Gestures and touches and kind words and deeds
Will bless every day that we live.

Judy Schwab